STAYING BULLY-FREE
ONLINE

A BULLY-FREE WORLD

Text by Pamela Hall
Illustrations by Bob Ostrom

magic
wagon

Content Consultant
Finessa Ferrell, Director,
National Center for School Engagement

visit us at www.abdopublishing.com

Published by Magic Wagon, a division of the ABDO Group, PO Box 398166, Minneapolis, MN 55439. Copyright © 2013 by Abdo Consulting Group, Inc. International copyrights reserved in all countries. All rights reserved. No part of this book may be reproduced in any form without written permission from the publisher.

Looking Glass Library™ is a trademark and logo of Magic Wagon.

Printed in the United States of America, North Mankato, Minnesota.
032012
112012

Text by Pamela Hall
Illustrations by Bob Ostrom
Edited by Holly Saari
Design and production by Craig Hinton

Library of Congress Cataloging-in-Publication Data

Hall, Pamela, 1961-
  Staying bully-free online / by Pamela Hall ; illustrated by Bob Ostrom ; content consultant, Finessa Ferrell.
      p. cm. -- (A bully-free world)
  ISBN 978-1-61641-849-6
  1. Cyberbullying--Juvenile literature. 2. Bullying--Prevention--Juvenile literature. I. Ostrom, Bob. II. Title.
  HV6773.15.C92.H35 2012
  302.34'302854678--dc23
                          2011038556

TABLE OF CONTENTS

CYBERBULLYING

Kids who bully want to feel powerful. They take power away from other kids by being mean to them. They want other kids to feel bad about themselves.

Bullying happens at school and on the playground. But there is also a new kind of bullying. Cyberbullying is using computers and cell phones to hurt other people. It is a simple way for kids to bully other kids because they aren't face-to-face with them. It is easy for them to send mean text messages. Follow along as the students at Niceville Elementary learn to stop cyberbullying.

BEING MEAN ONLINE

Cyberbullying can be social bullying. That is when people do or say mean things just to make others feel bad about themselves. Social bullying is even worse online because it can spread so quickly. More than half of kids and teens have been bullied online.

Tim checked his e-mail one day after school. Someone sent him a mean e-mail. But he couldn't tell who sent it because it was from a fake name. What can he do?

WHAT TO DO

Tim is really mad and hurt. But he shouldn't act on it. He should walk away from his computer for a bit. Then he won't respond by saying something mean back out of anger. If he did, he would become a bully, too.

Instead, Tim needs to report the e-mail to a parent. More than half of kids do not report cyberbullying. But Tim wants his mom to know. She can help Tim deal with the bullying.

HIDDEN IDENTITY

It is easy for kids to go online and not say who they are. They can easily make fun of another person when they don't think they can get in trouble for it. No one can see them through a computer.

Girls are more likely to be online bullies than boys. Sarah's friend Lee uses a fake name to write mean things about Joe online. Sarah feels bad. What can she do?

Joe is so gross! He never takes a shower. I would never be his friend!
Look what I wrote, Sarah. Hahaha!

WHAT TO DO

People who see bullying happen to another person have an important job to do. They must be an upstander and tell the bully to stop. They can do that by making the bully look silly. They can also make the bully feel bad about being mean. It is up to Sarah to step in and stand up for Joe!

SPREADING RUMORS

Another form of social bullying is spreading rumors. Joe texts all of his friends that Carlos eats food out of the garbage. What Joe is doing is wrong. It is never funny or fun to be bullied.

15

WHAT TO DO

    There are a couple things Carlos can do. First, he can ignore the rumor and walk away. He knows it isn't true. Second, he could make a joke about the rumor. He should only make a joke if he's okay with doing that.

EMBARRASSING PHOTOS

Lily took a picture of Ava with her phone. Ava had just come out of the bathroom. She had a long trail of toilet paper stuck to her shoe. Lily wants to send it to everyone in class. She doesn't like Ava and wants to embarrass her. Isabel sees the photo. What can she do?

WHAT TO DO

Isabel should help Ava by being an upstander. She should look Lily in the eyes and tell her to delete the picture. If Lily doesn't, Isabel will tell their teacher. Lily might be mad at Isabel for a bit. But Lily will probably delete the picture.

TAKE THE
BULLY TEST

How can you tell if you ever bully? You are a bully if you do things you know will hurt people or make them feel bad. Ask yourself these questions:

Q   Do I feel better when I hurt other kids or take their stuff?

Q   Do I use my strength or size to get my way?

Q   Do I like to leave others out to make them feel bad?

Q   Have I ever spread a rumor that I knew was not true?

Q   Do I like teasing others?

Q Is it funny to me when I see other kids getting made fun of?

Q Have I ever kicked, punched, or hit someone?

If you answered "yes" to any of these questions, you might be a bully. Is that really how you want to be?

Of course not! Everyone makes mistakes. You can change the way you act. The first step is to say, "I'm sorry." Practice being nice to other people. Think before you say or do something. Treat others the way you want to be treated.

NOTE TO PARENTS AND CAREGIVERS

Young children often imitate their parents' or caregivers' behaviors. If you show bullying actions or use bullying language, it is likely your children will, too. They do not know their behavior is unacceptable because they see it in trusted adults. You can help prevent your student from bullying by modeling good behavior

WORDS TO KNOW

cyberbullying—using technology such as the Internet and text messaging to bully others.

embarrass—to make someone feel ashamed or uncomfortable.

report—to tell an adult about being bullied.

rumor—talk that may not be true but is repeated by many people.

social bullying—telling secrets, spreading rumors, giving mean looks, and leaving kids out on purpose.

upstander—someone who sees bullying and stands up for the person being bullied.

WEB SITES

To learn more about bullying online, visit ABDO Group online at **www.abdopublishing.com**. Web sites about bullying online are featured on our Book Links page. These links are routinely monitored and updated to provide the most current information available.